The Spi

Other titles in *The Vision of . . .* series include:

Lament and Love: George Herbert
I Step, I Mount: John Henry Newman
Measureless to Man: Samuel Taylor Coleridge

The Spiritual Kiss

The Vision of St Aelred

Compiled by
Robert Van de Weyer and Pat Saunders

The Lamp
Press

Marshall Morgan and Scott
Lamp Press
34-42 Cleveland Street, London, W1P 5FB, U.K.

First published in 1989 by Marshall Morgan and Scott Publications Ltd
Part of the Marshall Pickering Holdings Group

ISBN: 0 551 01916 6

Text Set in Baskerville by Avocet Robinson, Buckingham
Printed in Great Britain by Courier International Ltd, Tiptree, Essex

The spiritual kiss is given and accepted, not by the touching of the mouth, but by the union of hearts and the mingling of spirits.

'Spiritual Friendship'

CONTENTS

[illegible]

[illegible] the [illegible]
[illegible] all the Christian saints [illegible]
[illegible] Richard Rolle [illegible]
[illegible] Church [illegible]
[illegible]

[illegible] Daniel [illegible]

[illegible]

[illegible] dreamy [illegible] which [illegible]
[illegible] legendary [illegible] England [illegible] pursued [illegible]
[illegible] life, and [illegible]
[illegible]

[illegible]

Introduction

Aelred of Rievaulx is amongst the most lovable and attractive of all the Christian saints: he deserves to stand alongside Mother Julian and Richard Rolle as one of the heroes of the mediaeval English Church. And yet few have heard of him, and fewer still have read his enchanting and profound books: indeed, there have been no popular editions of his works, and much of what he wrote has yet to be translated into modern English. When Aelred died, his close companion Walter Daniel anointed the index and middle fingers of his hands with sacred balsam, because 'with them he had written such sublime things about God'. Aelred's words radiate the same warmth and love, and the same sublime wisdom, to the modern reader as they did to his fellow monks eight centuries ago.

Aelred was born, probably in 1110, at the ancient abbey of Hexham in Northumbria. Since the Viking invasions the abbey church had stood in ruins, but Aelred's father, the last of a long line of married priests who had been guardians of the church, restored it to its former glory. Aelred was a dreamy, emotional child who loved to read the romantic legends of England's past and the lives of the Christian martyrs, and would often shed tears at the more moving scenes – a habit which he retained in later life, much to the consternation of other monks. When he was fourteen he met, by chance, David, who was soon to become King of Scotland, and who was visiting Hexham. David was instantly charmed by this handsome, quick-witted young man, and invited him to the Scottish Court to be a companion to his own two sons, Henry and Waldef.

Aelred's affectionate nature quickly made him popular amongst everyone at Court, and the friendships he formed with David and his sons were to last for the rest of their lives. Years later when he was abbot of Rievaulx he visited David each year; and when David invaded England, and his army threatened to overrun Rievaulx and the surrounding area, it was their mutual love which caused Henry to leave it untouched. Within a year in Scotland, Aelred's administrative ability had been recognised by David, who appointed him steward of the royal household, in charge of its entire domestic life. His success in this office and his popularity held the promise of a sparkling career.

But Aelred, despite his outward gaiety, was inwardly in turmoil. As a boy he had longed for intimacy, his heart flying from one passionate friendship to another, but now he found himself filled with sexual desire also. He fell in love with a young man at Court, and was horrified at what he regarded as the impurity of his feelings. To ease his agony he turned increasingly to religion, and his imagination was caught by stories of the new order of monks from Citeaux in France, who had recently begun setting up houses in Britain. Their rigorous way of life, recreating the simplicity of the first monastery of St Benedict, was profoundly attractive to his tormented soul. So, in 1134, when he was visiting Yorkshire on behalf of King David, he went to Rievaulx Abbey, the main Cistercian house. After a few short hours he was captivated by these austere monks in their grey and white habits; and, after a sleepless night staying in a nearby castle, he decided to offer himself as a novice.

After life at Court, Rievaulx was harsh, and at times Aelred was tempted to escape. But he began seeking comfort in reading the Scriptures; and the same passionate emotions he had felt for the young man at Court now turned to the person of Jesus Christ. He experienced Jesus as a warm, intimate friend who was by his side every minute of the day; and he found that, with Christ as the unseen companion, he could make friendships with other monks without fear of arousing his physical feelings. He began to enjoy the hard labour and sparse food of the monastery, and the same gaiety and good humour that had made him so popular at Court now returned, winning the affection of his fellow monks.

In 1143 he was appointed abbot at a new daughter house at Revesby in Lincolnshire, and four years later he was elected abbot of Rievaulx itself, a post he held until his death. By now Rievaulx contained over three hundred monks, and was a major force within the English Church. He was frequently invited to preach at synods and other church gatherings, he was asked to arbitrate in ecclesiastical disputes, and his advice was sought by both senior churchmen and by members of the English and Scottish Courts. Yet his first loyalty was to the spiritual needs of his brethren; and, however busy he was, he always found time to see those who wanted to speak to him. He could readily sympathise with every human weakness, being constantly aware of his own moral frailty; and, although he was firm and clear in the guidance he offered, his rebukes for those who fell short were always mild. He welcomed everyone who sought to join the monastery, however unsuitable they might appear, and under his gentle counsel many rough youths were turned into fine monks. His principle, which he frequently annunciated to those who questioned his liberal policy, was that 'no house is a true place of religion if it is too proud to bear with the weak and the foolish'. His position required that he showed no special favour, but he recognised his own continuing need for close friendship; so, despite some jealousy from other monks, he retained a few close companions, including Walter Daniel, an effeminate and highly emotional man whom Aelred described as 'fit to be loved, but not fit to be entrusted with positions of responsibility'.

Aelred had long been prone to arthritis and gall stones, and in his final years his body was so bent and twisted that Walter often had to carry him to church. A small wooden hut was built for him next to the infirmary where Walter cared for him. On days when the pain eased Aelred would ask young monks into his hut, inviting them to put questions to him on any matter which concerned them: he encouraged them to debate freely the points he made, but would conclude the meetings with a prayer in which any disagreement was offered to God to resolve. On Christmas Day, 1166, Walter carried Aelred into church where he delivered his last sermon. Throughout the following fortnight Walter remained with him constantly, reading the Scriptures and praying; and on the 11th January, 1167, with his head resting in Walter's arms, Aelred died.

* * *

Aelred wrote his first great work, *The Mirror of Charity*, at the request of St Bernard of Clairvaux, the spiritual leader of the Cistercian movement, whom Aelred had visited on a journey to Rome in 1142. On his return to Rievaulx, Aelred was appointed novice master, and *The Mirror of Charity* is full of practical advice for men struggling to adapt to the physical rigours of monastic life. Aelred describes his own experience as a novice, how he hated the sparse food, rough clothing and hard beds, and dreaded the bell which awakened the monks for the night office. But he compares the life of a monk to that of a true sportsman, such as a huntsman or hawker, who would endure any amount of hardship in pursuit of his prey; likewise, when the love of God possesses a man's heart, even the most extreme discomfort is bearable. And it is the call of divine love which is the central focus of the book. Aelred rejects the idea that holiness requires a person to suppress his natural emotions; on the contrary, in God's love man's emotions find their true fulfilment. Thus we have nothing to fear from passionate feelings for another person, so long as the ultimate object of that passion is God. And so he encourages his readers constantly to meditate on the person of Jesus Christ, to fly to 'the maternal breasts of Jesus' in times of trial, to read the stories of his life imagining oneself a companion at his side, and to feel towards him every emotion of love of which the human heart is capable. Only by this means can we find true spiritual peace – the peace which God himself experienced on the seventh day of creation, when he rested and saw that everything was good.

The Mirror of Charity contains all the themes which are to be found in Aelred's later works, and at times when he allows himself to write freely he rises to great heights of both literary and mystical expression. But too often Aelred is trying to conform to the scholarly conventions of his day, pressing his ideas into a philosophical framework to which they are ill-suited.

His second great book, *Spiritual Friendship*, which he worked at intermittently over many years, reveals the true Aelred: charming and humorous, yet also profoundly wise. His model is Cicero's *Of Friendship*, a book which he read as a teenager when trying to sort out his own turbulent emotions; and, like Cicero, he presents his ideas through a dialogue between himself and his pupils. But, whereas Cicero's conversations are mere questions and answers, in Aelred's work there is genuine debate; and, while Cicero was concerned only with philosophical matters, Aelred and his pupils speak of their own feelings and experiences.

The book consists of three conversations. The first is with a young monk, Yvo, whom Aelred notices looking sad at a meeting, and invites to talk. The second takes place some years later when Yvo has died: Aelred's close companion

Walter discovers Aelred's account of his conversation with Yvo – which Aelred had thought was lost – and Walter and another monk, Gratian, take up where Yvo left off. The central question is how a special friendship between two people can be truly Christian; and, since monastic teaching traditionally discouraged close personal friendships, there is the underlying question as to whether one should have friends at all. Aelred's reply is that if a friendship is truly spiritual, then both people will be carried upwards towards the friendship of Christ. A spiritual friendship must not be based merely on common likes and dislikes, nor should it have any ulterior motive; the bond should be a common desire to grow in the image of Christ. Thus in a true friendship rebukes are as welcome as praise, and there is total loyalty so that our natural swings of moods and emotions pose no threat to that mutual bond. At one point Yvo, excited by such a strong affirmation of his own feelings, suggests that one could adapt St John's famous verse, saying that 'God is friendship'; Aelred hesitates, but agrees that 'he who abides in friendship abides in God'.

Most strikingly, Aelred uses the image of a kiss to describe the union of two friends: 'in a kiss two spirits meet and mix and are united'. He says there are two kinds of kiss. The first is 'the bodily kiss made by the impression of the lips'. This is a natural sign of friendship, but should never be misused for 'carnal pleasure'. The second is 'the spiritual kiss', which is the natural affection that binds two hearts and since true affection is a gift of God, it is Christ who kisses us in our hearts.

By the time Aelred completed *Spiritual Friendship* he was already living in his hut next to the infirmary, with his beloved Walter tending him. It was during these final painful years that Aelred wrote his other major works. In *The Dialogue on the Soul* he develops the theme he had considered in *The Mirror of Charity*, that the soul is the mirror of God; and thus by looking inwards we can see the face of God. But it is in his *A Rule of Life for a Recluse* that we discover another facet of Aelred's literary gifts carried to perfection. For some time his sister, living as a hermit, had been pressing him to write a guide for recluses. Aelred finally responded, not by composing a practical rule of life, but rather by suggesting a method of private prayer. His scheme is wonderfully simple: it is to meditate on incidents in the gospels, imagining oneself personally involved, speaking to the other people present to understand their feelings and reactions, and observing Jesus at close quarters. At times, Aelred says, Jesus will seem to be avoiding you: 'he averts his eyes and closes his ears', so you find yourself crying out, 'why do you turn your face away from me?' But when he does come towards you the joy is all the greater, and his 'sweet love' flows into your heart.

* * *

To our knowledge, this present book is the first anthology of Aelred's works. Inevitably much of what he wrote seems obscure and irrelevant to the modern reader; yet equally, within all his books, there are passages which are a sheer joy to read – and it is these which we have selected.

The first chapter is a series of meditations, mostly taken from *The Mirror of Charity*, but also including Aelred's passage on 'the kiss' from *Spiritual Friendship*. The next two chapters are in the form of conversations, the first taken from his dramatic dialogue, *Spiritual Friendship*, and the second from his description of the life of a novice in *The Mirror of Charity*. Then comes Aelred's meditations on the life of Christ: these are mostly taken from *A Rule of Life for a Recluse*, but also include pieces from *The Boy Jesus at the Age of Twelve*, a short work he wrote for Yvo some years earlier, and from a sermon entitled *Martha and Mary*. Finally, there is a selection of prayers culled from all his writings, including his sermons. The prayers of the middle section are taken from *The Pastoral Prayer*, which he composed and used regularly during his years as abbot of Rievaulx; and the final prayer is Aelred's own final prayer uttered repeatedly during the last days of his life.

REFLECTIONS ON LOVE

Desire for the love of God

What is this love which I desire, O my God? Unless I am much misled, it is a wonderful delight in the soul, which is the more sweet for being unsullied by passion, more sincere if it is tender, and a source of joy when it embraces all our fellow men. Love may truly be called the heart's own sense of taste, since it enables us to feel your sweetness. Love is the eye by means of which we can see that you are good. Love is a capacity for God who transcends all things, and whoever loves God gathers God to himself. The more we love God, the more we possess him, simply because God *is* love: he is charity. Love is God's rich banquet, that so gratifies those who eat at his table and drink deep, that they forget and lose themselves, only to find themselves in him. And how shall this be done, unless they love him?

The sweetness of God's love

This feeling of the love of God is a great encouragement to good works for those who have been diffident about serving God. But for those whose lives are already dedicated to doing good, the sweetness of love comes as a necessary consolation when they tend to tire. And for those who have reached the heights of Christian perfection, the experience of love is a refreshment that cannot be taken away from them. Thus God, who is wonderfully merciful to us all, effects our salvation in these various ways. He draws us to himself with the delights of love, he warns us with his justice, and he enlightens us with wisdom. It is as if you were to try to convince someone who had never tasted it, that honey is the sweetest thing in the world. No one could be convinced by words alone. But as soon as God gives us a taste of even one drop of his sweet love, that taste creates such an appetite in our souls that we will do anything to have more of it. And whenever the labour involved in achieving our desire becomes too much, a little drop of the sweetness of love will restore our strength. Our merciful Saviour draws us to his salvation by the experience of his love, and leads us away from the temptations of the flesh; and this is more than reason or the fear of hell can do when temptation is very strong. He puts on us the yoke of his service, and we become so much attached to him that in the end we are made his simply by the delight of loving him, for every man is drawn by what delights him.

The peace of God's love

To some people it seems that perfect peace and stability are to be found in loving and being loved, and there is no denying this on condition that the love is rooted in God, and is for God's sake. For such a love is important and is to be encouraged. But friendships based on worldly values or rooted in lust give rise to nothing but envy, suspicion and jealousy which drive away all peace from the soul.

Perfect love finally brings its devotees to calm rest, and refreshes them with its delightful sweetness. But this can happen only when the body's death has finally conquered the allurements of the flesh, when the vision of God's own brightness has banished the darkness of error, and when the reverses of this world have been exchanged for the security of heaven.

When the land of our bodies has been rid of the savage beasts of passion, God lulls us into a heavenly sleep. And then the sea of God's brightness swallows us up in its vastness and carries us outside our own small compass, so that we see that the Lord is God.

This is the celebration of that Sabbath in heaven which will go on, as Isaiah tells us, for month after month, and for Sabbath after Sabbath. And when, one Sabbath, we have tasted as much of the initial stages of charity as the day allows, we shall be carried outside the bustle of this world into that unmarred Sabbath which no trouble can disturb and no bodily misfortune can hamper. Then, and only then, shall we love the Lord our God with all our heart and strength and by means of every virtue, and our neighbour as ourselves.

Love cannot be judged by feelings alone

Our love of God must not be gauged by the passing feelings we experience that are not controlled by the will, but rather we must judge them by the enduring quality of the will itself. For loving God means that we join our will to God's will. It means that our will consents to whatever the will of God commands. It means that we have only one reason for wishing anything, and the reason is that we know that God wills it.

The will, after all, is nothing if not love, so that when we speak of the will as being good or bad, we are thinking in terms of good love or bad love. God's will is God's love, and his will and his love are none other than the Holy Spirit, by whom charity is poured forth in our hearts. And this pouring out of love is simply the joining together of God's will with our own. As Saint Paul says, whoever cleaves to God becomes one spirit with him. For the Holy Spirit, who is the will and the love of God, so floods our human wills that he transforms them into himself, drawing them up to God and away from all that is beneath us. Thus the human will is made so to cleave to God that it becomes one spirit with the Holy Spirit, who is God.

The visitations of God's grace that come to us in the form of feelings and emotions, are for God to bestow when and where and to whom he wills. It is not for us to seek them, or even to ask for them, and if God should suddenly remove them from us, our wills must be in agreement with his. For the man who loves God is the man who bears patiently with all that God does to him, and who is zealous in carrying out God's precepts. If love were to be judged by feeling, this would mean that we only love God and our fellow men when we feel love towards God and towards our brethren.

The savour of love

Love takes its rise from feeling when we agree to let feeling guide us. It takes its rise from reason when our will consents to take reason as its guide. But a third love comes about when these three – reason, feeling and will – collaborate. The love that comes about through feeling is pleasant but it can be dangerous. It comes about through the experience of a pleasant attraction. The second, or reasonable one, is harder to achieve, but more fruitful. Reason compels the choice. The third is the best, and it has the full savour of real love. Love that is induced by mere feeling may well be good, but what we love in this way we love because it is pleasant, and nothing more. But in the full and perfect love which I placed last, we love not because it is pleasant to do so, but because it is the love of something worthy. Therefore it has its own sweetness and delight.

Love is governed by reason and affection

Love, as a gift of nature, is exemplified in the love of a mother for a child. Love as an obligation is, for example, the affection that arises as the result of the bestowal or acceptance of a gift. Love proceeds solely from reason when we love our enemies, when we love them not from a spontaneous movement of the heart, but under the compulsion of a precept. It proceeds only from affection when any person attracts another solely by his physical beauty, strength, eloquence and so on. Love has its source in reason and affection simultaneously, when he whom reason tells us is lovable for the beauty of his character, attracts us by the gentleness of his manners and the purity of his life. Thus, reason and affection are wedded, and jointly govern love: reason rendering it chaste, whilst affection makes it full of delight.

Love for ourselves

If we wish to love ourselves in the way God wants us to love ourselves, we must not be corrupted by the pleasures of the flesh. And in order that we be not overcome by these pleasures, the remedy is to turn all our love of the flesh to the flesh of Our Blessed Lord. Finally, in order to reach the state of perfect love for our fellow men, we must take even our enemies to our hearts. But we cannot remain in this perfect state unless we think always of the patience of Our Blessed Lord and Saviour in his sufferings.

A spiritual Noah's ark

Let us imagine our heart to be a kind of spiritual Noah's Ark, made of the imperishable wood of virtues and good deeds. There we shall find various compartments on different levels made ready for the different kinds of people we shall meet. Just as Noah had to look after wild beasts, we have to find room in our hearts for those who are out for our blood – our enemies, that is, who hate us. We can give them our prayers, and any temporal help we can, but only after we have seen to the needs of those more closely connected with us. Let us, then, leave the lower floor and the outbuildings for our enemies, and keep the inner rooms and the upper floors for those nearer to us. The animals which are not wild but are still none the less earthly and unclean (let us say domestic animals, and crawling things) come next. These are not carnal and bloodthirsty men, and they have nothing against us. Their needs come next, and they deserve our prayers, our encouragement, and occasionally our correction. Of these, some may be connected with us through ties of blood, or of gratitude, which give them a claim to our intimacy. On the top floor, where Noah lodged his family, we can put those who have nothing in common with the beasts, being neither given to anger nor lust nor uncleanness. They are typical men whose desires do not yet carry them higher than a human ideal of perfection. And among these, we must take to us more especially those who are near to us by family ties, or by friendship, or by deeds of kindness. The topmost floor of all being reserved to Noah's birds, we must find a place there for those whom we know to be specially near to God, flying up to heaven, as it were, on wings of virtue, above the normal state of men. And here again, we shall find that there are some special few of this number who are more closely allied to us than others, those, that is, for whom we have a most special place in our hearts, whose companionship is particularly dear to us and whom we cherish more sweetly and embrace more ardently in our hearts. But above all these there is a place reserved for the one who is above even the highest of our acquaintances, and that is Jesus, Our Lord, who made the Noah's ark of our hearts in the first place, and repaired it after it had fallen in ruin. All that is beneath him he gathers to himself, and transfuses into all things his own sweet savour, his light and his splendour, drawing everything to his own love. He alone, in all these, above all these, takes all our love to himself, demanding it for his use alone. He makes his dwelling over all else in our hearts, and in the very depths of our souls.

The friendship of Christ

Out of perfect charity we often love those who are a burden, and a source of suffering to us. And though we treat them with all courtesy, sincerity, frankness and goodwill, yet we do not make them our intimate friends. With friendship, on the contrary, we find courtesy joined to genuine friendliness, sincerity to amiability, frankness to sympathy, goodwill to deeds. All these have their source in Christ. The transition from friendship to the love of God, looked at in this light, does not appear difficult or unnatural. We pass from Christ, who inspires us with love for our friends, to Christ, who offers himself as a friend. In this way, human love gives place to divine love, emotional delight is exchanged for spiritual delight, affection for man is transformed into affection for God. So does a man, clinging to his friend in the spirit of Christ, become one heart and one mind with him. And he moves upward through the different degrees of love until he attains the friendship of Christ and is made one spirit with him in one kiss.

The spiritual kiss

Let us consider, for a moment, the qualities of an earthly kiss. In a kiss, two spirits meet, commingle, and become one; and, as a result of this action, there arises in the mind a wonderful feeling of delight that awakens and binds together the affection of them that kiss.

There is, therefore, according to the different kinds of union, a kiss of the body, a kiss of the spirit, a kiss of the mind. The kiss of the body is made by the impress of the lips; the kiss of the spirit by the union of the hearts; the kiss of the mind by the infusion of grace into the soul through the Holy Spirit of God.

Hence, the bodily kiss is not to be given or accepted save for certain and just reasons. For instance, it may be given as a sign of reconciliation, in the case of enemies who become friends; as a sign of peace, such as is given by those about to receive Holy Communion in Church; as a sign of love, such as that between bride and bridegroom or between friends who have been long absent; as a sign of Catholic unity, such as should be given at the welcome of a guest.

The spiritual kiss really pertains to friends. It is given and accepted, not by the touching of the mouth, but by the union of hearts and the mingling of spirits. In it, the Spirit of God himself is present, so that everything connected with it is chaste, and the joy that ensues proceeds from him. This kiss, I should like to call, the Kiss of Christ, a kiss which he gives, not by his own mouth, but by the mouth of another. For in the two friends it creates such a holy feeling of delight that there seems to be but one soul in two bodies. And they feel moved to cry out with the prophet, 'Behold how goodly and pleasant it is for brethren to dwell together in unity.'

When, therefore, the mind has become accustomed to this kiss, and recognises that all the delight ultimately has its source in Christ, it says, as if musing with itself, 'O, if only he himself would come'. And in that utterance it aspires to the kiss of the mind, and immediately cries out, 'Let him kiss me with the kiss of his mouth.' So when all earthly affections have been disengaged, and all earthly desires and thoughts have been extinguished, the soul finds rest and delight only in the kiss of Christ, surrenders to His embrace, exults, and murmurs, 'his left hand is under my head, and his right hand shall embrace me.'

The consolation of friendship

The sweetness of God that we taste in this life is given us, not so much for enjoyment as for a consolation and encouragement for our weakness. That is why it is such a great joy to have the consolation of someone's affection – someone to whom one is deeply united by the bonds of love; someone in whom our weary spirit may find rest, and to whom we may pour out our souls . . . someone whose conversation is as sweet as a song in the tedium of our daily life. He must be someone whose soul will be to us a refuge to creep into when the world is altogether too much for us; someone to whom we can confide all our thoughts. His spirit will give us the comforting kiss that heals all the sickness of our preoccupied hearts. He will weep with us when we are troubled, and rejoice with us when we are happy, and he will always be there to consult when we are in doubt. And we will be so deeply bound to him in our hearts that even when he is far away, we shall find him together with us in spirit, together and alone. The world will fall asleep all round you, you will find, and your soul will rest, embraced in absolute peace. Your two hearts will lie quiet together, united as if they were one, as the grace of the Holy Spirit flows over you both. In this life on earth we can love a few people in this way, with heart and mind together, for they are more bound to us by the ties of love than any others. Our Lord Jesus Christ is our example in this too, for we know that there was one whom he loved above all the rest. If anyone should look askance at such a love, let him remember how Jesus came to take pity on us, transforming our love by showing us his. He showed us that love by giving his heart as a resting place for one head in particular. This was a special sign of love for the beloved disciple, given to one alone, not to all. All were loved equally, no one doubts it, but for Saint John he had a special love, as we can see by the name he gives himself, 'the disciple whom Jesus loved'.

A garland of love

The day before yesterday, as I was walking round the cloisters, all the brethren sat together, grouped like a most lovely garland. And I gazed on them, as Adam must have gazed on the leaves and the trees and flowers and fruits amidst the delights of Paradise. And in the whole of that throng I could not find one whom I did not love, and by whom I was not loved. And I was filled with such great joy that it surpassed any delight that this world could give. For I felt as if my spirit was transfused into all of them, and their affection was reciprocally flowing into me. And I felt that I could sincerely say with the prophet – 'behold how goodly and pleasant it is for brethren to dwell together.'

CONVERSATIONS ON FRIENDSHIP

The Origin of Friendship

Aelred is visiting Warden Abbey in Bedfordshire, and has been speaking with a large group of brothers. Amongst them is Yvo with whom Aelred shares a special closeness and understanding. Yvo detaches himself from the group and asks to speak with Aelred alone so that he may disclose to him the deep feelings of his heart without disturbance.

Aelred: Here we are, then, just the two of us; and Christ, I hope, makes the third. There is no one at the moment to disturb us. No one can break in upon our quiet talk. We are quite alone, beyond the reach of noise and din of voices.

So come, Brother, and open your mind to me. Tell me all that is troubling you, and let us make the most of this unique opportunity.

Yvo: May I suggest that you speak to me on spiritual friendship? Tell me, what is its nature and practicability? What is its source? What is its purpose? Can it exist between all types of men; and if not, between whom?

How can it be uninterrupted through life and how brought into abiding harmony with the pursuit of holiness?

Aelred: I am surprised that you should ask me such questions. Surely you know that the most celebrated teachers of ancient times discussed these matters at great length. You must have spent some of your early years in studying these things. Have you never read Cicero's book on friendship? He there analyses in detail, and describes in his own inimitable style, all its salient characteristics, besides making some rules about it.

Yvo: Yes, I know the book quite well. But ever since I acquired a taste for Holy Scripture and conceived a love for the name of Jesus, everything else I hear or read, no matter how beautifully expressed, seems insipid and ineffectual. That is why I should like to see Cicero's ideas or at least the few of them that can further our purpose, proved on the authority of Scripture. I should like to know how genuine friendship has its source in Christ, how it is promoted by Christ, and how it is referred both as to its aim and utility, to Christ. It is quite clear to me that Cicero has not sounded the real depths of friendship. How could he, when he was completely ignorant of Christ, its source and its ultimate goal?

Aelred: You could not have made a more profound or truer statement about friendship than that it has its source, its continuance, and its fulfilment in Christ. Come then: What question shall we approach first?

Yvo: I think that we ought to discuss the nature of

friendship first; otherwise, we shall be talking at random.

Aelred: Very well. Do you accept Cicero's definition of it – 'Friendship is agreement on things sacred and profane, accompanied by goodwill and love.'?

Yvo: Yes. If it satisfies you, I am quite willing to agree with it.

Aelred: Well then, I take it that all who share the same opinions on matters sacred and profane, who have the same likes and dislikes, and who are united by mutual love and goodwill, enjoy perfect friendship?

Yvo: I see no objection. But what did Cicero mean exactly by the words 'love' and 'goodwill'?

Aelred: Perhaps, by the word 'love' he signified the heart's affection; and by 'goodwill', the expression of it in deeds. For agreement on things sacred and profane should be heartfelt on both sides, that is, it should be acceptable, welcome to both. And the expression of it in exterior action should be pleasing and full of goodwill.

Yvo: I must confess that the definition appeals to me. But it can hardly be applicable to pagans, Jews and bad Christians. For it is my firm conviction that between those who are without Christ, there can be no true friendship.

Aelred: It will soon become evident where the

definition fails by under or over-statement. For the moment we must accept it, or condemn it altogether. It may not commend itself to you as a perfect definition; but if it enables you to understand what friendship is, it will have served its purpose.

* * *

Yvo: Do you mind if I ask you now to explain to me the meaning of the word 'friendship'?

Aelred: Not at all, provided you make allowance for my ignorance. I cannot be expected to tell you what I do not know myself. The word 'friend' (amicus) then is derived as far as I am aware, from a word 'amare' meaning 'to love' and, 'friendship' from the word 'friend'. So friendship has to do with love. Now love is an appetite of the rational soul by means of which the soul ardently seeks its object, yearns to possess it, relishes it when possessed, and embraces it without letting it go.

This love has a guardian, namely, one's friend. He must keep faithful guard over that love, otherwise he will not keep strict guard over all its secrets. For his duty is to heal all one's moral wounds – to bear with all one's defects. He has to rejoice when one is joyful, grieve when one is sorrowful.

In a word, he has to embrace all his friend's interests as if they were his own.

Friendship, therefore, is a virtue by which two hearts are united and made one, in the bond of sweetness and love. For this reason, the philosophers of this world have classed friendship not with the perishable and fleeting things of time, but with the virtues that last for ever. Solomon undoubtedly takes the same view when he says in the Book of Proverbs, 'He that is a friend loveth at all times'. Clearly showing that friendship, when it is true, is eternal, and only perishes when it is not true.

* * *

Yvo: Are we to admit then, that there is no distinction between friendship and charity?

Aelred: There is, indeed, a great difference. We know without any shadow of doubt, because it is God's will, that charity is of more universal application than friendship. For by the law of charity we are urged to love not only friends but enemies also. But the name of 'friend' is applicable only to those who enjoy our complete confidence, and share all our secrets; and they on their part are closely united to us on the same understanding of trust and confidence.

Yvo: There are many living in the world, I am afraid, whose basis of agreement with one another seems to be passion rather than virtue. And not infrequently they place more value on the pleasure such intimacies afford than on all the amenities of life. I hope therefore you will not be annoyed if I call one of these many friendships 'spiritual'. This will differentiate it from the rest, with which it is in some way involved, and by which it is somewhat obscured. It will stand out by comparison more prominently, and its beauty appear more desirable, and it will make it easier for those who are seeking to recognise it.

Aelred: Men who are attracted to one another by passion have no right whatever to be called friends. Friendship is based on love, and a man who does not love cannot be a friend.

The friendship which is definitely genuine is spiritual. It is not motivated by any earthly consideration nor by any self-seeking. It is cultivated for its own intrinisic worth and because it satisfies the fundamental needs of the human heart.

The advantages and rewards to be gained from spiritual friendship are itself: nothing else. That is why Our Lord said in the Gospel, 'I have chosen you to go and bring forth fruit': that is, to love one another. True friendship grows ever deeper and deeper; and its fruit consists in the enjoyment of its full perfection. Where such a friendship exists, there indeed is indentity of likes and dislikes. And the more sincere it is, the greater is the pleasure experienced; the holier it is, the more blessings are received. Where men have this love, they want no evil: they want everything good. Such friendship, in other words, is directed by prudence, ruled by justice, preserved by fortitude, moderated by temperance. It is the very antithesis of the sensual attachment.

* * *

Aelred: If you closely examine the claims we made for friendship, I think you will find that it has so many likenesses to wisdom, that I dare assert – friendship is nothing else but wisdom.

Yvo: You surprise me. But you will not find it easy to convince me of it.

Aelred: No? Have you forgotten that passage of Scripture, 'He who is a friend loveth at all times'? And the maxim of St Jerome, 'Friendship that can cease was never genuine'? I have already proved, I think, beyond cavil, that friendship cannot long continue without charity. Since then we find in friendship the freshness of eternity, the refulgence of truth and the fruitfulness of charity, why should we refuse the name wisdom to these three?

Yvo: What idea is this you are putting into my head? Am I to say of friendship, what John the friend of Jesus said of charity, 'God is Friendship'?

Aelred: It does sound most unusual, doesn't it? And there is no authority for it in Scripture. But I would not hesitate to attribute to friendship anything that is predicated of charity, as for instance, 'He who abideth in friendship, abideth in God and God in him'.

The Advantages of Friendship

Years have passed, and Yvo has died. The manuscript containing Aelred's conversation with him is lost, and no further dialogues have been recorded.

Walter, a brother at Rievaulx Abbey (who later became Aelred's biographer) has news that the lost manuscript has been found. Its discovery inspires many thoughts and questions on friendship in Walter's mind, and he comes to Aelred to discuss them.

Walter: Tell me, do you remember that conversation you had with Yvo at one time on spiritual friendship, or have you forgotten it? Can you recall any of the questions he proposed to you, or the conclusions you arrived at? Do you remember how much of it you wrote down afterwards?

Aelred: Yes, I do. The memory of Yvo, of his presence and his sympathy, are so fresh in my mind, that although he has passed from this world to his eternal rest, yet I can never bring myself to think of him as dead. He is ever present in my heart. I seem to see there his grave and holy countenance, I can hear his pleasant words. And it seems that, either I have passed to a better world, or he is still dwelling with me in this vale of tears. I jotted down all the answers to his questions on spiritual friendship.But, as you know, I lost that paper many years ago.

Walter: But I know where it is! And to tell you the truth, the whole reason for my excitement and impatience is this. Three days ago that very document was found. And I have learned from several people that it was handed over to you. Do let me see it, please! I shall not rest until I have examined it, and found out exactly how much is needed to complete it. If I think there are any other questions to be answered, or any further suggestions to be made, I shall place them before you, Reverend Father, and you can reject, approve, or explain them as you wish.

Aelred: Very well then. As you wish. But I agree only on the condition that you read it privately. I do not wish you to make it public in case I decide that certain sections are to be cut out, others amplified or corrected.

* * *

Walter: My eagerness to hear what you have to say is all the greater because what I read in your script was most delightful. Your discussion on the nature of friendship was eminently practical. I wish you would now tell me what advantages may be expected by those who cultivate it. For you appear to have proved its fundamental importance with arguments so telling that the better its advantages and aims are recognised, the more enthusiastically will it be sought after.

Aelred: Friendship is true glory to the rich, is home to the exile, money to the poor, medicine to the sick, life to the dead, beauty to the strong, power to the weak, reward to the toiler. Such great honour, remembrance, praise, and desire surround friends that their life is esteemed worthy of praise and their death is precious in the sight of the Lord.

And to crown all this, friendship is a means to perfection, is indeed only a degree short of perfection. For from being a friend of man, one becomes a friend of God – according to the saying of Our Lord, 'I will no longer call you servants, but friends'.

Walter: I must confess that your description moves me so deeply and attracts me so strongly towards friendship that, if I am deprived of so great a good and so many advantages, I do not think I shall be able to live. The idea of friendship as the best means of attaining perfection is wonderful. I am completely overcome by it, almost snatched by it from earth to heaven.

But would you please explain the idea more fully to me?

. . . Hullo! Who comes here? Gratian, I do believe, a real devotee of friendship, if I may say so: a man whose whole aim in life is to love and be loved.

Gratian: You are too kind brother. I am most grateful to you for allowing me to thrust in upon you uninvited and to join in your spiritual conference.

But if you are in earnest, and have called me a devotee of friendship not merely for a joke, but in all seriousness, then I ought to have been called in at the beginning of this talk. That would have saved me this confusion, and given a decent appearance to my eagerness.

However, please go on, Father, from where you left off. Set the table again for this spiritual repast, so that even if I cannot be filled like Walter (who has eaten up practically everything and invited me to the leavings) yet I may be refreshed a little.

Aelred: Have no fear, my son. There are so many things in friendship, still to be discussed, that, if a wise man were to continue this talk from this point, you would imagine we had said nothing.

* * *

Walter: I should be glad if you would make a definite statement about the ideal one should have in cultivating friendship.

Aelred: Christ himself has fixed the ideal to be attained in friendship. 'Greater love than this no man hath,' he says, 'than that a man lay down his life for his friend.' That is the limit to love between friends. They should be willing to die for one another. Does that satisfy you?

Gratian: Well, since there can be no love greater, I suppose it will have to be sufficient.

Walter: But what if some wretched pagans or sinners become so closely attached to one another that they were willing to die for one another? Would you say that they had attained the ideal friendship?

Aelred: God forbid! Friendship cannot exist between sinners.

Gratian: Tell us, then. What type of people can take up and continue a friendship?

Aelred: Briefly, the rule is this. Friendship may take root between two good people, may develop between the really virtuous, but may only reach its highest level between the perfect. For as long as anyone takes delight in evil, as long as he loves the pleasures of sense more than purity, licentiousness more than self-control, flattery more than reproof, he cannot aspire to friendship.

Friendship has its root in virtue. And if its source remains a mystery to you, it is difficult, nay, impossible for you to experience it, even in its rudimentary stages. For the love that makes dishonourable demands upon a friend is base, and utterly unworthy of the name 'friendship'. Yet if a man's inclination to sin is not subdued and restrained, he must inevitably descend to such a course of action whenever he is tempted or enticed.

Hence the opinion that declares that loyalty and honourable conduct are to be set aside for the sake of a friend, is most reprehensible. To say that one has sinned for the sake of a friend is no excuse for the sin.

Gratian: Well, what is the use of friendship to us? We are not particularly good ourselves.

Aelred: I am not so exacting in my standard of 'good' as some. They consider no man good unless he has reached perfection. I call a man good if he lives soberly, justly and piously in this world; if he asks no one to commit a wrong deed, and refuses to commit one himself when asked. It is my conviction that friendship can really flourish between such men.

Walter: I must say that my sentiments almost coincide with those who say that friendship is, as a general rule, to be avoided. It seems to abound with pain and care, and is beset with a hundred difficulties and trials. Surely, each man has enough troubles of his own, and has no need of implicating himself in the worries and cares of other people. Besides, nothing is more difficult than to remain a friend until death. Yet it is contemptible to begin a friendship and then to break it off. For this reason, a commendable opinion seems to be that it is safer so to love a man that, if you wish, you can afterwards hate him. In this case, you are able to keep your hold on the reins of friendship, and tighten them whenever you feel inclined.

Gratian If that is so, Reverend Father – if it is so easy to discourage anyone from seeking after friendship, the enjoyment of which you have been commending as holy, profitable, pleasing to God and a means to perfection – then we have been wasting time, you in talking, we in listening. If his opinion is to prevail – that one can love today and hate tomorrow – then, a man can be a friend to all and loyal to none. He will praise today and blame tomorrow. One day he will flatter, another day he will backbite. He will be as ready to kiss as to revile. To all appearances his friendship will be as easy to win as to lose.

Walter: Sorry! I thought doves had no bile! However, tell me, if you can, how this opinion, which seems to gall Gratian so much, can be refuted.

Aelred: Cicero has some splendid ideas on this topic. 'Those men,' he says, 'who ban friendship from their lives, remove, as it were, the sun from the earth, because, of all God's gifts to men, it is the most beautiful and the most pleasing.'

What kind of wisdom is it that inspires a man to cast friendship aside for the sake of avoiding a little worry and anxiety and fear? No virtue can be acquired or preserved without toil. Surely you must realise from your own personal experience that prudence cannot struggle against error, nor temperance against unlawful desires, nor justice against wrong-doing, nor fortitutde against sloth, without toil.

* * *

Gratian: How are we to judge whether a friendship is unworthy or not?

Aelred: To please you, I will briefly describe the types of friendship we ought to avoid.

First of all, there is the childish friendship. For the most part, it is based on unstable and ill-regulated affections, and lacks all discernment. It is unreasonable, fickle, intemperate, and quite regardless both of convenience and danger. For a short time, it is very violent: it binds its votaries closely together and affords them great plesure. But affection without reason is a mere animal passion, and liable to fall into the worst excesses, since it is unable to distinguish between what is right and what is wrong.

The foundations of spiritual friendship are pure intention, sound judgment and self restraint. Within these limits the most tender love may be indulged, and the greatest delights may be experienced.

There is another type of friendship based on the mutual gratification of evil passions. But I decline to speak of it. Friendship is far too good a name for it.

There is, besides, a friendship whose source is the consideration of personal gain. Many there are who think that on this account, it should be courted, fostered and embraced. But once we give entrance to this view, see the result: we must obviously rule out all those who have no possessions. They may be quite worthy of our love, but we must deny them the enjoyment of our friendship because we cannot hope to gain any temporal advantage from them.

Walter: It seems to me that many allow themselves to be deceived by false appearances. What ought we most of all to avoid? What kind of friendship ought we to desire, to cultivate, and embrace?

Aelred: The reward of friendship is itself. The man who hopes for anything else does not understand what true friendship is. Only those who have been rapt by it wholly into God, and have been completely absorbed in contemplation of him, know what that reward is. For the benefits which friendship confers are many and great. But we must recognise that they do not engender friendship; friendship, on the contrary, engenders them.

In the case of good men, then, friendship comes first, and as a consequence, mutual advantage ensues. But what brings joy to the heart is not so much the friend's gift as the friend's love.

The Perfecting of Friendship

It is the following day, and Walter and Gratian return to continue their conversation with Aelred.

Aelred: Hullo! What has brought you today?

Gratian: I am surprised you should ask, Reverend Father. Surely you do not need reminding.

Aelred: Ah, yes, of course not. Is Walter not with you?

Gratian: I'm afraid not. Anyway, he can't complain that we are late.

Aelred: Shall we go on with the discussion?

Gratian: I think we had better wait for him. I find him a great help. He is quicker at understanding, sharper at questioning, and he has a more tenacious memory than I have. (*At this point, Walter comes in*).

Aelred: Did you hear that, Walter? Gratian is more friendly towards you than you imagined.

Walter: Well, why shouldn't he be? He is friendly towards everybody. But, to turn to another subject, we have remembered your promise and are both ready. Let us make the most of our opportunity.

Aelred: Very good. Now the source and origin of friendship is, as we have said, love. You may have love without friendship, but not friendship without love. Love proceeds from nature or from obligation. It can spring from reason alone, or from affection alone; or from both at once.

There are four stages by which perfect friendship is attained: first choice; second, probation; third, acceptance; fourth, supreme agreement on all matters spiritual and temporal, with accompanying love and goodwill.

Walter: Gratian will have to set us a good example, and then we shall be able to see whether in himself, and in his friend, those four conditions are fulfilled. We shall see how far he agrees with the other's tastes, how far he is willing to do or forego what is unjust, immoral or distasteful.

But enough of this. We are eagerly waiting to hear what you have to say about the four stages of friendship which you mentioned a few moments ago.

Aelred: Let us treat of choice. There are certain defects of character which render a man simply incapable of fulfilling the requirements of friendship for any length of time. Don't choose that type of man. But if his behaviour and demeanour are otherwise pleasant, treat him with great circumspection because in time you may be able to cure his failing and make him a fit recipient for your friendship. I have in mind – to name a few – the irascible; the inconstant; the distrustful; and the talkative.

It is very difficult for a man who is irascible not to turn against his friend at some time or other.

Walter: And yet, unless we are greatly mistaken, you used to be friendly with an irascible man. We have heard it said that he often injured you, and yet, to the day of his death, you never said an unkind word to him.

Aelred: Some people are by nature irascible. But by constant effort they are able to restrain and hold this passion in check so that they never fall into any of the five faults that break off or destroy friendship. Still, they are, at times, an occasion of suffering to their friends through their inconsiderate words and intemperate zeal.

If we make friends with such people, we must bear patiently with them. And since we are convinced of the genuineness of their affection, we must allow them some latitude in speech and action. When they do commit a fault, we should admonish them gently without showing irritation.

Gratian: There is one member of the community whom you appear to love more than any of us, and a few days ago he did and said something in anger which he must have known was most displeasing to you. Yet as far as we can see, you have not changed your attitude towards him. This has caused us not a little surprise, because, as we have been saying, you never fail to gratify his wishes, no matter how trivial they are; and yet, for your sake, he will not endure the slightest inconvenience.

Walter: Gratian is a good deal bolder than I am. I knew all about this, too. But I did not presume to mention it, because I knew your affection for the man.

Aelred: The monk you mention is certainly most dear to me; and now that I have accepted him as a friend, I cannot withold my affection from him. If, on the one hand, I am more self-controlled than he when we happen to have differences of opinion, this is because I always find it easier to subdue my own will than to subdue his. When there is no danger of wrong-doing, no confidences broken, no principle at stake, I always give way to him. It is easy to endure his excesses. And when his peace of mind is threatened, it costs me little to fall in with his views.

Walter: The first man, of course, is dead now. But I hope the other one has apologised to you for his rudeness – though, really, it does not concern me.

* * *

Aelred: We must beware of the fickle and suspicious. One of the greatest blessings of friendship is the enjoyment of a deep sense of security in entrusting yourself and your concerns to a friend. But how can you repose in this security if he falls in with everyone's opinion and changes his mind with every breath of wind like a weathercock? How can you be sure of him if his character is as soft as wax – receptive of every impression that men can stamp on it? If there is anything really essential to friendship, it is a consciousness and feeling of security, and a profound peace of heart.

As for the talkative individual, I think he should not be chosen as a friend; for 'the man of tongue shall not be justified'. 'Shouldst thou see,' says the wise man, 'anyone swift to speak, there is more hope of a fool than of him.' For this reason, you should choose a friend who is not troubled by anger, shaken by inconstancy, made restless by distrust, or frivolous in his talk. It is particularly advisable to choose a man whose behaviour and status are in harmony with your own. Between persons of different character, as St Ambrose says, 'there can be no friendship'.

Walter: But wherever are we going to find a man who is neither irascible, nor inconstant, nor suspicious? I will not mention the other failing, because we are talkative, that's quite evident.

Aelred: True. It is not easy to discover a person who is immune to all these pests. Still, there are usually many who are able to rise above them. They are able to check anger by patience, to curb unseasonable jocularity by due gravity, to drive away mistrust by reflecting on the constancy of love. When I commended some as more fit for friendship than others, it was of these I was thinking: for they have overcome their passions by the contrary virtues, and are more to be relied on. This is to be expected, since they are more accustomed to resisting temptations of all kinds.

Gratian: Would you be angry with me if I were to venture a remark? It is this. That friend of yours whom we mentioned a short time ago, and whom we know you are fond of – is he what you would call an irascible person?

Aelred: He is, certainly. But not as a friend.

Gratian: What do you mean by saying that he is not irascible as a friend?

Aelred: Well, you agree that we are friends, don't you?

Gratian: Certainly.

Aelred: Did you ever hear of anger, quarrels, disagreements, rivalries, or disputes between us?

Gratian: Never. But we always attributed this to your patience, not to his.

Aelred: That is where you make a mistake. If affection cannot curb anger, patience never will: for patience, instead of quietening an angry man, rouses him to greater fury. If you answer an angry man with insult and reproach, he likes it, and it brings him peace. The man you are speaking of is so meticulous about preserving all the conventions of friendship that, when he is greatly upset and on the point of blurting out insolent remarks, I am able to restrain him with a mere glance. He never makes unpleasant comments in public, and no matter how troubled he is, he always waits until we are alone before relieving his feelings. If he acted like this more from temperament than from friendship, my appreciation of his character would suffer a decline. But, as a matter of fact, when we disagree on some specific point, we always renounce selfish interests. The result is that sometimes he follows my wishes instead of his own; and sometimes I place his preferences before mine.

* * *

Walter: I must confess that I am still inclined to the opinion that one can live more peacefully without friends.

Aelred: That is surprising. Life without friends is life without pleasure.

Walter: Why is that?

Aelred: Well, suppose the whole human race had been withdrawn from the earth, and you were the only person left behind. You would be in sole possession of all the pleasures and riches of the world – the gold and the silver and the precious stones, the walled cities, the turreted castles, the spacious halls, the sculptures and the paintings. And on this supposition you would be in man's primitive state, with everything subject to your dominion – the sheep and the oxen, and the cattle of the field, the birds of the air and the fishes of the sea, which throng the ways of the sea. But do you think you would be happy if you had no companion to share it with you?

Walter: Certainly not.

Aelred: Suppose, now, you had a companion. But you did not understand his language nor his habits, and consequently had no knowledge of his thoughts and feelings.

Walter: I think if I could not get on friendly terms by signs and dumb play, I would rather have no one at all.

Aelred: Suppose, on the other hand, you had someone with you, whom you loved very deeply, and who returned your affection; would not that change the whole complexion of things, so that what before was bitter, would now become sweet and pleasant?

Walter: Of course.

Aelred: And the more friends you had like him the happier you would be, isn't that so?

Walter: Yes.

Aelred: Well, this is the great and wonderful happiness that awaits us in heaven. God has created between himself and his creatures, between the manifold orders and degrees of angelic spirits, between the innumerable types of saints, an all-embracing friendship, so that each one loves the others as himself. The result is that, as each individual rejoices in his own happiness, so he finds joy in the happiness of his neighbours; and the beatitude of each individual is the beatitude of all, and the sum total of the beatitude of all is enjoyed by each individual. In that blessed world, no one hides his thoughts or conceals his affection. There, abides that true and everlasting friendship. It begins in this world, but it reaches perfection in the next. Let heaven, then, be your ideal. Choose your friends on that model, friends I mean, whom you love as your own self, who are completely in your confidence, to whom you can lay bare all your innermost thoughts, and who are firm, staunch and steadfast in all circumstances.

Do you think that any mortal man exists who would not desire that friendship?

Walter: No, I hardly think so.

Aelred: But what if you saw a man in the midst of his companions, mistrusting them all, fearing them as if they were plotting against his life, withholding his love from them because he felt that no one loved him? Would you not consider him to be the most wretched?

Walter: Most wretched, certainly.

Aelred: Then you must agree that the happiest man is he who finds perfect rest in the affections of those around him; who loves all who come in contact with him, and feels he is loved by them; who goes his way unruffled by any fear or mistrust.

Walter: Yes, that is very true.

Aelred: But, of course, even if we cannot realise this state of things in this world, since it is reserved for us in the next, we must count our happiness by the number of our friends.

* * *

Aelred: But now the sun is going down, and I must bring this discussion to a close. But before I do so, remember this. Friendship is rooted in love. A man who does not love himself cannot possibly love another, for the love he offers his neighbour must be framed on the kind of love he has for himself. It is evident that he does not love himself if he commits base and immoral actions for himself.

Consequently, the primary obligation that binds any man is to keep himself chaste, to deny himself the indulgence of his passions, and to procure for himself every spiritual advantage. When he has made this the rule of self-love, let him follow the same rule in love of his neighbour.

This kind of love, however, can be extended to a multitude of men. So let him choose out a particular man with whom he can share his innermost hopes and aspirations, and to whom he can show his affection. Then he can lay bare to him all his longings and ambitions, and the deeper thoughts and intentions of his heart. The choice of such a man should be guided not by the impulse of feeling, but by the sane judgment of reason, and should be grounded on similarity of tastes and the recognition of sterling qualities.

After this, a man may with safety surrender

himself to friendship, but sincerely and without frivolity, not forgetting that a man is not completely trustworthy until his faithfulness, uprightness and patience have been put to the test. Afterwards he may be entrusted little by little with your confidence, made participant in your ideals and pursuits, and rendered conformable to you in outlook. For, friends should be so like one another, that as soon as one sees the other, the likeness of one's countenance should be transformed into that of the other, whether it be dejected with sorrow, or smiling with pleasure.

Then there is prayer which they offer up for each other – which is so much the more efficacious in so far as it is made to God with deeper sincerity and earnestness, accompanied, as it is, at times, with tears of fear or love or sorrow.

In this way, a man praying to Christ for his friend, and yearning to be heard for his friend's sake, fixes his attention on him with care and desire. And, suddenly and insensibly, his affection changes to another affection, and experiencing, as it were, at closer quarters the sweetness of Christ, he begins to taste how sweet he is, and to feel how kind he is.

And thus, beginning with the love with which he embraces his friend, and rising to the love with which he embraces Christ, he will happily enjoy the spiritual delight of friendship, awaiting the fulness of all that is to come, when all fear and anxiety for one another, which we experience now, will be taken away; when all trials which we now bear for one another will be driven afar off, and the sting of death which now afflicts us and makes us grieve for one another, will be destroyed. And then in complete security we shall rejoice for the everlasting existence of the Highest Good, when this friendship, to which on earth we admit but few, will be extended to all, and by all will be extended to God, since God will be All in all.

CONVERSATION WITH A NOVICE

Novice: Why is it that in my previous worldly life I received more spiritual consolation than I do in the monastery?

Aelred: Let me ask you first if you think the life you led in the world was holier and more acceptable to God than the way of life you follow in the monastery?

Novice: No, that is far from the case. If in those days I had done any of the things I now do, all my friends would have thought me a saint!

Aelred: In those days did you ever consider how St Paul tells us we must go through many tribulations to get to the kingdom of God? And has it every occurred to you that not even a just man may lift up his head, since he is filled with affliction and misery?

Novice: Why, no, I have never thought about such ideas; rather I am conscious of deeply loving Christ.

Aelred: And did you suffer as much for Christ's sake in those days as you do now as a novice?

Novice: In those days I would not have tolerated for a

single hour the mortifications I bear daily in the monastic life. I would never, for instance, have spent a whole day in absolute silence. Far from it. I used to spend my whole life just chattering about this and that. I did weep real tears when I thought of how much I loved Christ, but that didn't stop me from going straight back to my usual amusements: the company of friends and relatives, eating too much, drinking too much, sleeping late into the day, giving way to every feeling of anger or discontent, fighting, coveting other people's property, and indulging my own will in every way.

Aelred: Describe, by contrast, the life you lead as a novice.

Novice: That's easy enough! Just look at me! My clothes, for instance – they are so rough. The food I eat, by comparison with what I used to eat, is unbearably coarse, and all I have to drink now is water. As for sleep, I spend as much time nodding into my books as I do on my bed! And when I go to bed I am utterly worn out, but just at the very moment when sleep is pleasantest and I feel I could go on sleeping for hours, the bell rings for matins.

There is no place for self-will and no time for idleness. But at the same time you cannot help realising that there are so many good things to make up for what is hard. We never quarrel, for instance. We are never angry with one another, never have the poor coming to complain that we are defrauding them of their rights. We never get involved in litigation of any sort, and there is peace everywhere here, silence and calm. We are completely free from the tumult of the world. There is such unity among the brethren, so much concord, that everything belongs to everyone. And what I love above everything else is that there is no consideration of persons for the rank they held in the world, for birth makes no difference here. We are only treated differently according to our needs – if we are ill, for instance, or not very strong. The fruits of our common work are divided among all, with nothing extra for favourites, but only those in need. It is absolutely marvellous to me that in this monastery three hundred men can obey the commands of one superior, and do everything he says as if they had all agreed among themselves on this one thing, or as if they had heard the voice of God telling them to do it. In fact I seem to find here every perfection that the Gospel precepts contain, and everything I read in the teaching of the fathers and of the monks of old.

Aelred: Since you are a novice, I can put all this enthusiasm down to fervour, and not to self-satisfaction! But you must be careful to remember that there is no perfection in this life that may not be cleverly aped by people who are insincere. And I don't want you to be put off by them, when you discover frauds in the religious life, as you certainly will. But tell me, now that you have described the monastic life in such detail, is it to be compared with those precious tears which you wept in the world?

Novice: Heaven forbid that my conscience should be calmed by a few tears, or that tears alone should take away the fear of the last judgement! Only now, in this monastery, am I at peace in my soul, and so can look forward calmly to the time when God will take me. But do you think it better to consider as worthless all the tender feelings of love I used to experience in the world, and all the tears I shed for the love of Christ?

Aelred: No, no, that is far from being the case. Indeed, in their way these tears and feelings are extremely useful. But, you must remember not to judge your love for God by these passing feelings and emotions, since a good performance on the stage can move us to tears.

Novice: How true. That is exactly what used to happen to me when I heard them telling the story of King Arthur. And now I think of it, I sometimes feel quite proud of myself when I am moved to tears by the story of our Lord's sufferings in the Gospel or in a good sermon. But I can see now how stupid it is if I give way to vainglory for the sake of passing emotion, just as I used to when I listened to romances. But you were saying, if I remember, that feelings and tears could be useful in some way. In what way do you mean?

Aelred: I mean that these things will give you some knowledge of the truth, so that you may come to know yourself and may learn not to spare your own faults. Such feelings and tears will, in fact, show you not that you are wonderfully holy, but that you are weak and needy.

Do you not see that your fervent conversion and present austere way of living are the fruit of your original contrition? These are the outcome of your tears. God used your sorrow to work out your salvation. Therefore is it surprising that when your deep feeling of contrition has done its work, it should disappear? The work you have now in hand is that of suffering all for Christ's sake, to exercise the virtue of patience, to overcome the overbearing flesh with vigils and fasts, to bear temptations without giving in to them, and to call away your soul from everything that savours of the world.

With the virtue of obedience you must mortify your will; and whenever you are wearied by the labours of your present state of life, you must go to Jesus by means of sincere prayer to draw, as it were, the milk of consolation from the breast of him who is a mother to you. In the beginning of your conversion you were given the sweet feeling of God's love in order to draw you away from evil. And after that you will find that consolation comes to refresh you on your way, so that you may not be overcome by this hard life. Finally, when you have mastered the many trials and difficulties that give you trouble at the moment, you will find that great abundance of sweetness which is laid up for those that fear the Lord.

Novice: I hope to God that it will all come to pass as you have said, for I already know the sweetness of God's love as it comes at the beginning of the soul's conversion. Also I am beginning to realise how consolation comes during the souls's trials in order to give it comfort on the way. And I trust that I shall one day also experience the great abundance of God's sweetness. Just the thought of it brings tears to my eyes.

Aelred: At least you see how differently things in fact turn out from the way you had visualised them.

Novice: How do you mean?

Aelred: You have discovered that you love God much less than you thought you did. I mean that it is precisely when you thought that you loved God most that you find you loved him less. The more negligent we are of our salvation and the more our souls are weak, the more imperfect our love is, don't you agree? And now that you know yourself a little better, you discover that God sends his consolations in the first place to show us the error of our ways; and when we have accepted the fact that we are at fault, and amend our lives, consolation helps us not to be overcome by the weariness of that amendment. But in neither case is love perfect.

Novice: Yes, they are sadly mistaken who part with their salvation so easily by refusing to give up things that are bad. If they could only experience a little of the love you have been speaking about, not only would they be offered forgiveness for their past sins, but they would also be given more of the same delight in God's love. Yet often the encouragement that God gives us to abandon our evil lives profits us nothing. It makes us feel a little holier, perhaps, but we go back to our bad ways none the less, and even a little more determinedly than before. Then although we have been given by God a spirit of remorse, our eyes still do not see, nor do our ears hear. There is, I suppose, a sort of remorse that makes us blind, and deaf as well, since we imagine that tears alone are enough to wash away our sins, when in fact we must prove our sorrow by works of penance.

Aelred: Tears are something very precious to God, and they are sufficient sacrifice to atone for all our past sins, but only if we are truly penitent and confess our sins, and with a contrite spirit fly to Jesus and do all we can to make amends. For how can there be true penance if we return to our evil ways? And therefore you, who are a novice, must work out your salvation with labour and care, with mortification of the flesh, with vigils and manual work, with poor food and rough clothes, with silence and recollection. These will make an acceptable sacrifice of your whole being – both the inner and the outward man – and tears will enkindle the flame of charity that it sends up to God.

MEDITATIONS ON THE LIFE OF CHRIST

Here are some seeds of spiritual meditation which I have made it my business to sow for you concerning the memory of Christ's boons, to the end that from them a rich crop of the love of God may spring up and grow to maturity. Meditation will arouse the affections, the affections will give birth to desire, desire will stir up tears, so that your tears may be bread for you day and night until you appear in his sight and say to him what is written in the Song of Songs: 'My Beloved is mine and I am his.'

Nativity

First enter the room of blessed Mary and with her read the books which prophesy the virginal birth and the coming of Christ. Wait there for the arrival of the angel, so that you may see him as he comes in, hear him as he utters his greeting, and so, filled with amazement and rapt out of yourself, greet your most sweet Lady together with the angel. Cry with a loud voice: 'Hail, full of grace, the Lord is with you, blessed are you among women.' Repeat this several times and consider what this fullness of grace is in which the whole world shared when the Word was made flesh and dwelt among us, full of grace and truth. Wonder at the Lord who fills earth and heaven being enclosed within the womb of a maiden.

Next, with all your devotion accompany the Mother as she makes her way to Bethlehem. Take shelter in the inn with her, be present and help her as she gives birth, and when the infant is laid in the manger break out into words of exultant joy together with Isaiah and cry: 'A child has been born to us, a son is given to us.' Embrace that sweet crib, let love overcome your reluctance, affection drive out fear. Put your lips to those most sacred feet, kiss them again and again.

Next contemplate the shepherds' vigil, wonder at the angelic host, make your own contribution to their heavenly melody, singing both with your heart and with your lips: 'Glory be to God on high, and on earth peace to men of good will.'

Do not omit the Magi and their gifts from your

meditation, nor leave the Child unaccompanied on his flight into Egypt. Accept as true the legend that he was captured by robbers on the way and owed his escape to a young man who is supposed to have been the son of the robber chief. After seizing his booty he looked at the Child in his Mother's bosom and was so impressed by the majesty that radiated from his beautiful face as to be convinced that he was something more than man. Inflamed with love, he embraced him and said: 'O most blessed of children, if ever the occasion arises to take pity on me, then remember me and do not forget the present moment.' This is said to be the thief who was crucified at Christ's right hand and rebuked the other thief when he blasphemed.

So, in order to kindle love I consider it worthwhile to accept this legend as true, without making any rash assertions as to its authority.

Boyhood

Further, do you not think you will gain some devotion by contemplating him at Nazareth as a boy among boys, obedient to his mother and helping his foster-father with his work?

Consider him too at the age of twelve going up to Jerusalem with his parents. It was the Jews' custom that when they went up for the feast-day, men and women travelled apart so that no defilement should make its way in, since God's Law prescribed that only the clean should take part in the sacred rites. We may imagine then that on that journey the boy Jesus granted the sweetness of his presence now to his father and the men with him, now to his mother and the women in whose company she was. Let us consider, I beg, how great was their happiness to whom it was given to see his face for so many days and to hear his words, sweet as honey; to contemplate in a human being, in a boy, certain signs of heavenly powers shining forth, and to intersperse their conversations with reflections on the mystery of the wisdom which saves. The old are amazed, the young are lost in admiration, and boys of his own age are kept from mischief by the seriousness of his behaviour and the weight of his words. For I think that the grace of heaven shone from that most beautiful face with such charm as to make everyone look at it, listen to him and be moved to affection. See, I beg, how he is seized upon and led away by each and every one of them. Old men kiss him, young men embrace him, boys wait upon him.

When they all arrive in the Holy City having enjoyed this pleasure, watch, I beg, the devout and holy competition there is between one family and another as all are anxious to be granted his most lovable and charming presence. Happy the one who wins. Perhaps it was for this reason that, when the celebrations were over and they set about their return, the boy Jesus stayed on in Jerusalem without his parents' knowledge. For everyone thought that he was with someone else, since he was loved by all and sought for by all, and his parents did not know that he was not there until, at the end of a day's journey, they looked for him among their kindred and friends, going from family to family of those who had gone up with them.

It is with good reason then that at the end of the three days he was found in the temple, in the midst of the doctors and elders. As he had revealed the loving design of God the Father for men's redemption to the angels and the saints no longer in the body, as it would seem, so he began gradually to manifest the same in the most sacred of all places in the world, the temple at Jerusalem, and to those in the first place who were the guardians of this most precious treasure, the promise contained in Scripture. First listening and asking questions, then answering questions, he unfolded the most sacred mysteries. Then, we read, 'all were amazed at the wisdom of his answers.' This is an example of humility and modesty for boys and youths, teaching them to be silent in the midst of their elders, to listen and ask questions so as to learn.

Join his Mother in looking for him during those three days. What a flood of tears will you not shed when you hear his Mother scolding her Son with the gentle reproach: 'Son, why have you dealt so with us? Behold, your father and I have been looking for you in sorrow.'

'How is it,' he said, 'that you sought me? Did you not know that I must be concerned with my Father's business?' Here already he begins to disclose the secret of the heavenly mysteries in which he had been occupied for the three days. In order to give a more clearly defined and outstanding example of humility and obedience, and at the same time of readiness to give up one's own will and comply with the injunctions of elders even to one's own disadvantage, he disengaged himself from these sublime concerns, so useful and so necessary, to submit himself to the will of his parents: in the words of the Evangelist, 'He went down with them and was subject to them.'

Ministry

Our Lord dedicated for your benefit the solitude of the desert and sanctified fasting, to teach you that it is there you have to engage the crafty foe in battle. Consider that this was done for you and in your stead; and meditate on the way in which it was done and imitate what was done.

Then call to mind the woman who was taken in adultery and what Jesus did and said when he was asked to give sentence: he wrote on the earth, in order to show them up as of the earth rather than of heaven, and then said, 'Let him among you who is without sin be the first to throw a stone at her.' But when the words struck them all with terror and drove them out of the temple, imagine how kind were his eyes as he turned to her, how gentle and tender was the voice with which he pronounced his sentence of absolution. Think how he would have sighed, how he would have wept as he said: 'Has no one condemned you, woman? Neither shall I condemn you.' Happy was the woman, I feel inclined to say, in this adultery, forgiven as she was for the past and assured for the future. Good Jesus, when it is you who say, 'I will not condemn,' who else will condemn? When it is God who justifies, who is there who will condemn? Yet the words which you added must not be overlooked: 'Go, and do not sin any more.'

Now go into the Pharisee's house and see our Lord in his place at table there. Together with that most blessed sinner, approach his feet, wash them with your tears, wipe them with your hair, soothe them with kisses and warm them with ointments. Are you not already penetrated with the fragrance of that sacred oil? If he still will not let you approach his feet, be insistent, beseech him, raise your eyes to him brimming with tears and extort from him with deep sighs and unutterable groanings what you seek. Strive with God as Jacob did, so that he may rejoice in being overcome. It will seem to you sometimes that he averts his gaze, closes his ears, hides the feet you long to touch. None the less be insistent, welcome or unwelcome, and cry out: 'How long will you turn your face away from me? How long shall I have to cry out without your listening to me? Give back to me, good Jesus, the joy of your salvation, for my heart has said to you: "I have sought your face, your face; Lord, I will seek".'

Do not pass by that house in which the paralytic was let down through the roof to Jesus, where kindness and power came to meet one another. 'My son,' he said, 'your sins are forgiven.' What amazing clemency, what unspeakable mercy. That happy man received forgiveness of his sins without having asked for it, without any preliminary confession, without having carried it by any satisfaction, without any contrition that might seem to call for it. It was bodily health he asked for, not that of the soul, yet he received health of both body and soul.

This is the power of Christ's unutterable mercy, and as it is blasphemous to deny it, so it is the height of folly to presume on it. He can say and do to anyone he wills the same as he said and did to the paralytic: 'Your sins are forgiven.' But anyone who expects that this will be said to him, without any toil or contrition or confession or even prayer on his part, will never be forgiven his sins.

Martha and Mary

Come to Bethany, where the sacred bonds of friendship are consecrated by the authority of our Lord. For Jesus loved Martha, Mary and Lazarus. There can be no doubt that this was on account of the special friendship by which they were privileged to be more intimately attached to him. That is borne out by those sweet tears with which he associated himself with the mourners and which all the people interpreted as a sign of love: 'See,' they said, 'how he loved him.'

'And behold they gave him a supper there at which Martha was serving, while Lazarus was one of those at table with him. Now Mary brought ointment in an alabaster box and breaking the alabaster poured the ointment out upon Jesus' head.' Be glad, I beg of you, to take part in this meal. Mark carefully the part played by each of them. Martha was serving, Lazarus was reclining at table, Mary poured out ointment.

Recognise the state of these two sisters, Martha and Mary. The one was busy, the other was at leisure. The one gave, the other asked. The one was anxious to serve, the other nourished her affections. She did not walk about or run hither and thither, was not concerned with the reception of guests, nor distracted by household worries, nor busy with answering cries of the poor. She just sat at Jesus' feet and listened to what he had to say.

Both these women live in the house of your soul: one to sit at Jesus' feet that she may hear his words, the other to wait on him that he may eat. If Mary alone is in that house there would be no one to feed the Lord. Therefore, Martha signifies that action by which man labours for Christ. Mary, however, signifies that rest by which man, freed from corporal works, delights in the sweetness of God through reading, prayer, and contemplation. In no way should you neglect Mary on account of Martha, nor Martha on account of Mary. For if you neglect Martha, who will feed Jesus? If you neglect Mary, what does it matter that Jesus entered your house, when you taste nothing of his sweetness?

Break then the alabaster of your heart and whatever devotion you have, whatever love, whatever desire, whatever affection, pour it all out upon your Bridegroom's head, while you adore the man in God and God in the man.

Passion

But now we must rise and go hence. Where to? you ask. To be sure, to accompany the Lord of heaven and earth as he rides on an ass; to marvel at the great things which are done on your behalf and mingle your praise with that of the children, crying out: 'Hosanna to the Son of David, blessed is he who comes in the name of the Lord.'

Now then go up with him into the large upper room, furnished for supper, and rejoice to share the delights of the meal which brings us salvation. Let love overcome shyness, affection drive out fear, so that he may at least give you an alms from the crumbs of that table when you beg for something. Or stand at a distance and, like a poor man looking to a rich man, stretch out your hand to receive something, let your tears declare your hunger. But when he rises from table, girds himself with the towel and pours water into the basin, consider what majesty it is that is washing and drying the feet of men, what graciousness it is that touches with his sacred hands the feet of the traitor. Look and wait and, last of all, give him your own feet to wash, because the man whom he does not wash will have no part with him. And when he commends his disciples to the Father in that most holy prayer and says, 'Father, keep them in thy name,' bow your head, so that of you too it may be said, 'I wish that where I am they too may be with me.'

It is good for you to be here, but we must depart. He himself leads the way to Mount Olivet, do you follow. And although, taking with him Peter and the two sons of of Zebedee, he withdraws into solitude, look on if only from a distance and see how he takes upon himself our weakness. See how he to whom everything belongs begins to be dismayed and afraid: 'My soul is ready to die with sorrow,' he says.

But here comes the traitor, followed by a crowd of the godless, and as Judas offers his kiss they lay their hands on your Lord. They hold him, make him fast and tie those sweet hands with bonds. Who could endure such behaviour? I know your heart now is filled with pity, you are set on fire with indignation. Let him, be, I beg, let him suffer, for it is on your behalf he is suffering. Why do you long for a sword? Why are you angry? If, like Peter, you cut off someone's ear, amputate an arm or a foot, he will restore it and without any doubt he will bring back to life anyone you may kill.

Follow him rather to the courtyard of the High Priest and bathe with your tears his most beautiful face which they are covering with spittle. See with what loving gaze, how mercifully, how effectually he looked at Peter who has thrice denied him and now turns, comes to his right mind and weeps bitterly.

But now it is morning and he is delivered over to Pilate. There charges are brought against him and he says nothing, because he is led to slaughter like a sheep, and like a lamb before the shearer he has not opened his mouth. Mark well how he stands before the governor: his head bent, his eyes cast down, his face serene, saying little, ready for insults and scourging. I know you can bear it no longer, that you will not be able to look on while his most sweet back is torn with whips, his face struck, his majestic head crowned with thorns, that right hand which made heaven and earth mocked with a reed.

See now, after the scourging he is led forth wearing the crown of thorns and the purple robe. Pilate says: 'Behold the man.' Indeed he is a man. Who could doubt it? The weals left by the rods witness to it, the open wounds, the spittle which defiles him.

The judge has taken his place at the judgment seat, the sentence has been pronounced and already the doomed man is led off to death carrying his own cross. O what a sight. Do you see? Behold princely power is upon his shoulder. This is the sceptre of justice, the sceptre by which he reigns. He is given wine mixed with gall. He is stripped of his garments and they are divided amongst the soldiers. The tunic is not torn but is given whole to the one designated by lot. His sweet hands and feet are pierced with nails, he is stretched out on the Cross and hung up between two thieves. The Mediator of God and men hangs midway between heaven and earth, unites the heights with the depths and joins the things of earth to the things of heaven. Heaven is aghast, earth marvels.

And what of you? It is not surprising if when the sun mourns you mourn too, if when the earth trembles you tremble with it, if when rocks are split your heart is torn in pieces, if when the women who are by the Cross weep you add your tears to theirs. However, amid all this consider what tranquillity was preserved in that most sweet breast, what loving kindness it exhibited. He pays no attention to the wrongs done to him, takes no notice of the pain, disregards the insults, but rather has compassion on those who are making him suffer, heals those who are wounding him, wins life for those who are killing him. With what sweetness of disposition, with what devotion of spirit, in what fullness of charity he cries: 'Father, forgive them.'

Then one of the soldiers opened his side with a lance and there came forth blood and water. Hasten , linger not, eat the honeycomb with your honey, drink your wine with your milk. The blood is changed into wine to gladden you, the water into milk to nourish you. From the rock streams have flowed for you, wounds have been made in his limbs, holes in the wall of his body, in which, like a dove, you may hide while you kiss them one by one. Your lips, stained with his blood, will become like a scarlet ribbon and your word sweet.

But wait yet a while until that noble councillor comes to extract the nails and free his hands and feet. See how in his most happy arms he embraces that sweet body and clasps it to his breast. Then could that holy man say: 'My beloved is a bundle of myrrh for me, he shall rest upon my breast.' It is for you to follow that precious treasure of heaven and earth, and either hold the feet or support the hands and arms, or at least gather up carefully the drops of the precious blood as they fall one by one and wipe the dust from the feet. See also how gently, how solicitously blessed Nicodemus handles his limbs, rubbing ointments on them, and then with holy Joseph wraps them in the shroud and lays them in the tomb.

Resurrection

Do not fail subsequently to keep Magdalene company, remember to visit with her your Lord's tomb, taking with you the perfumes she has prepared. If only you might be found worthy to see in spirit what she saw with her eyes, now an angel sitting on the stone that has been rolled away from the entrance, now inside the tomb one angel where his head had lain, one where his feet, proclaiming the glory of his Resurrection, now Jesus himself looking with so gentle a gaze on Mary as she weeps for sorrow, and saying to her with so sweet a voice: 'Mary.' What could be sweeter than this utterance? What could be more tender? What more delightful? 'Mary.' At this utterance let all the floods burst forth, let tears stream up from the very bottom of your heart, let sighs and sobs issue from your inmost depths. Tears preclude any further utterance as the voice is stifled by emotion, and excess of love leaves the soul dumb, the body without feeling.

'Do not touch me,' he says. What a harsh command, now intolerable: 'Do not touch me.' How is this, Lord? Why may I not touch you? May I not touch, may I not kiss those lovable feet, for my sake pierced with nails and drenched in blood? Are you less gentle than usual because you are more glorious? But I will not let you go, I will not leave you, I will not spare my tears, my breast will burst with sobs and sighs unless I touch you.

His answer is: 'Fear not, this boon is not refused you but kept until later. Only go and tell my brethren that I have risen.' She runs quickly, anxious to return quickly.

She returns, but together with other women. These Jesus comes to meet with affection, restoring their spirits and banishing their sadness. And notice, the boon is now given which had previously been kept until later for they came close and clasped his feet.

Linger here as long as you can. Do not let these delights of yours be interrupted by sleep or disturbed by any tumult from without.

PRAYERS

Gospel Prayers

Blessed are you among women

O sweet Lady, with what sweetness you were inebriated, with what a fire of love you were inflamed, when you felt in your mind and in your womb the presence of majesty, when he took flesh to himself from your flesh and fashioned for himself from your members members in which all the fullness of the Godhead might dwell in bodily form.

Behold God with us

Behold Emmanuel, behold God with us. How can he be more with me? He is little as I am, weak as I, naked and poor as I. In all things he has become conformed to me. He has taken what is mine and given what is his. I lay as one dead. There was no voice in me. I was without feeling and the light of my eyes was gone. Today that great prophet came down, mighty in word and work. He placed his face upon mine, his mouth upon my mouth, his hands on my hands and he became Emmanuel – God with us.

I found him whom my soul loves

Tell me, my dearest Lady, Mother of my Lord, what were your feelings, your surprise, your joy, when you found your dearest son, the boy Jesus, not among boys but among teachers, and beheld the gaze of all eyes bent on him, everyone eagerly listening to him, while the little and the great, the learned and the ignorant alike told of his wisdom and of the answers he gave?

'I found,' she says, 'him whom my soul loves. I held him fast and would not let him go.' Hold him fast, dearest Lady, hold fast him whom you love, cast yourself upon his neck, embrace him, kiss him and make up for his absence during three days with increased delight.

Holy Nazareth

O Nazareth, holy, blessed, and lovable city, beautiful and fruitful city, more beautiful than heaven and more fruitful than paradise. In you a tree has sprung up, beautiful to behold, smooth to touch, and sweet to taste. Its fruit brings not death but eternal life. I am not forbidden but invited to taste it. Holy Nazareth, you are dearer to me than paradise. In you the old is renewed, the ruined repaired, the withered revived and the decayed made to bloom again.

You have filled the hungry soul

Who will grant me, good Jesus, to follow in your footsteps and so to run after you that eventually I may overtake you? I, yes I, am that prodigal son who took to himself his share of the inheritance, for I did not wish to preserve my strength for you, and set out for a distant land, the region of unlikeness, behaving as one of the dumb beasts and made like them. There I squandered all I owned in riotous living and so I began to feel want. Unhappy want, not only lacking bread but unable even to profit by the food of pigs. Following the most unclean of animals I wandered in the desert, in a waterless country, searching in vain for the way to a city I could dwell in. Hungry and thirsty, my soul wasted away in suffering. Then I said: 'How many hired servants in my father's house have bread in abundance, while here I perish for hunger?' While I thus cried to the Lord he hearkened to me and led me into the right path, so that I might make my way to a city I could dwell in. What city, but that which abounds in bread and is called the House of Bread, Bethlehem? May your mercies praise you, Lord, for you have filled the empty soul, and the hungry soul you have filled with good things.

Your weakness is my strength

O Lord Jesus, I will embrace you who became a little child for me. In my weakness I clasp you who became weak for me. A mere man, I embrace the God made man, the God who became a man as poor as I am, and came into Jerusalem seated on a humble donkey. I embrace you, O Lord, because your lowly state is my greatness, and your weakness is my strength. The foolishness of God is my wisdom.

A safe place for sinners

Kiss, kiss, kiss, blessed sinner, kiss those dearest, sweetest, most beautiful of feet, by which the serpent's head is crushed, before which the old enemy is cast forth, by which vices are trodden down, before which all the glory of this world bows; those feet which tread with admirable power on the necks of the proud and the lofty. Kiss, I say, those feet, press your fortunate lips to them, so that after you no sinner may be afraid of them, no one, whatever crimes he has committed, may flee from them, no one may be overcome by the consciousness of his unworthiness. Kiss them, embrace them, hold them fast, those feet venerated by angels and men alike. Apply to them the ointment of repentance and confession, so that the whole house may be filled with the fragrance of the ointment. Thanks be to you, blessed sinner, for showing the world a safe place for its sinners, the feet of Jesus, which despise no one, reject no one, repel no one, welcome everyone, admit everyone.

May my soul embrace you

O Lord Jesus, I beg you to allow my soul to grow wings in the nest of your teaching. May my soul embrace you who was crucified for me, and drink the lifegiving draught of your most sweet blood. May the thought of you and of your passion obsess my memory, lest the fog of forgetfulness blot out the thought completely. Until I come before your face I will shun all knowledge except that of my crucified Lord, lest the untruth of error upset the sound foundations of faith. May all my love be directed to your love, instead of seeking after its own useless desires. I pray, with David, that the very ends of the earth may be mindful of the Lord, and I turn to him, so that I may not seem to ask these blessings for myself alone.

Pastoral Prayers

Good Shepherd Jesus

O Good Shepherd Jesus, good, gentle, tender Shepherd, behold a shepherd, poor and pitiful, a shepherd of your sheep indeed, but weak and clumsy and of little use, cries out to you. To you, I say, Good Shepherd, this shepherd, who is not good, makes his prayer. He cries to you, troubled on his own account, and troubled for your sheep.

A prayer for my ministry

To you, my Jesus, I confess; to you, my Saviour and my hope, to you my comfort and my God, I humbly own that I am not as contrite and as fearful as I ought to be for my past sins; nor do I feel enough concern about my present ones. And you, sweet Lord, have set a man like this over your family, over the sheep of your pasture. Me, who takes all too little trouble with myself, you bid to be concerned on their behalf; and me, who never prays enough about my own sins, you would have pray for them. I, who have taught myself so little too, have also to teach them. Wretch that I am, what have I done? What have I undertaken? What was I thinking of?

O Lord, I lay my prayers before you, trusting not in my own righteousness, but in your great mercy; and where no merit of my own can lift its voice, duty is eloquent.

Let your eyes, therefore, be upon me, Lord, and let your ears be open to my prayers.

A prayer for my own needs

Lord, look at my soul's wounds. Your living and effective eye sees everything. It pierces like a sword, even to part asunder soul and spirit. Assuredly, my Lord, you see in my soul the traces of my former sins, my present perils, and also motives and occasions for others yet to be. You see these things, Lord, and I would have you see them. You know all, O Searcher of my heart, that there is nothing in my soul that I would hide from you, even had I the power to escape your eyes. So see me, sweet Lord, see me. My hope, most Merciful, is in your loving kindness.

I ask you, by the power of your most sweet name, and by your holy manhood's mystery, to put away my sins and heal the languors of my soul, mindful only of your goodness, not of my ingratitude. Lord, may your good, sweet Spirit descend into my heart, and fashion there a dwelling for himself.

A special prayer for wisdom

My God, you know what a fool I am, my weakness is not hidden from your sight. Therefore, sweet Lord, I ask you not for gold, I ask you not for silver, nor for jewels, but only that you would give me wisdom, that I may know to rule your people well.

O font of wisdom, send her from your throne of might, to be with me, to work with me, to act in me, to speak in me, to order all my thoughts and words and deeds and plans according to your will and to the glory of your name.

A prayer for the good of all

You know my heart, Lord; you know that my will is that whatever you have given your servant should be devoted wholly to their service, and spent for them in its entirety; and I myself, moreover, would be freely spent for them. So may it be, O Lord, so may it be. My powers of perception and of speech, my work time and my leisure, my doing and my thinking, the times when things go well with me, the times when they go ill, my life, my death, my good health and my weakness, each single thing that makes me what I am, the fact that I exist and think and judge, let all be used, let all be spent for those whom you did deign to be spent yourself.

Teach me your servant, therefore, Lord, teach me, I pray you, by your Holy Spirit, how to devote myself to them and how to spend myself on their behalf. Give me, by your unutterable grace, the power to bear with their shortcomings patiently, to share their griefs in loving sympathy, and to afford them help according to their needs. May my words and teaching build them up, and may they always be assisted by my prayers.

A prayer for my brothers

Hear me yet further, God most merciful, for those whom I am compelled and drawn to pray to you both by my duty and by my heart's love. Remembering your kindness, I am bold. Hear me, hear me, O Lord my God, and let your eyes be open on them day and night. Spread your wings, most loving Lord and shield them; stretch forth your holy right hand, Lord, and bless them; and pour into their hearts your Holy Spirit, that he may keep them in unity of spirit and the bond of peace, chaste in their bodies, lowly in their minds. May he be there to help them when they pray, and fill them with the unction and riches of your love.

Be in their midst, according to your faithful promise. And, since you know what each of them needs, I pray you, strengthen what is weak in them, spurn not their frailty, heal that which is diseased, give joy for sorrow, kindle what is lukewarm, establish what is insecure in them, that each of them may know he does not lack your grace in any of his trials and temptations.

A prayer for our temporal needs

Lord, as you shall see fit, provide your servants also with those temporal goods whereby the weakness of this wretched body is in this life sustained. This one thing only do I crave, my Lord, from your sweet pity: namely, that whether it be much or little that you give, you would make me, your servant, a good and faithful steward in respect to all, a wise and fair distributor, a sensible provider. Inspire them too, my God, to bear it patiently when you withhold things; and, when you do bestow, to use your gifts with temperance and restraint.

Inspire them, O Lord, also to have of me, who am your servant, and their servant for your sake, such an opinion as may profit them, such love and fear of me, as you, Lord, see to be good for them.

Into your holy hands

I, for my part, commit them into your holy hands and loving providence. May no one snatch them from your hand, nor from your servant's, unto whom you have committed them. May they persevere with gladness in their holy purpose, unto the attainment of everlasting life, with you, our most sweet Lord, their Helper always, who live and reign to ages of ages. Amen.

Personal Prayers

How great is your mercy

O sweet Lord, what shall I give you back for all you have given me? How sweet and gentle is your spirit in every way! For great is your mercy towards me, since you have stretched out your hand from above to free me from the power of my enemies and from the danger of drowning in the flood. And you have snatched my soul from the depths of hell from the very moment when I first tasted your sweetness there, hearing your voice as if it came from afar.

A still small voice

Good Jesus, the water of your doctrine flows in silence. Your teaching is not poured into ears by an eleoquent tongue but is breathed into hearts by your sweet spirit. Of you it is written: His voice will not strain, nor shout. It will not to be heard abroad. Inside it is heard, within the heart it is heard, it is heard in silence.

The sweetness of my Lord

Your sadness, Lord Jesus, means more to me than all the joys of the world. The tears you shed at the death of a friend are sweeter to me than the fortitude of philosophers who think a wise man ought not to be moved by affection. Sweeter to me is your food and drink in the midst of sinners and publicans than the rigid abstinence of the Pharisees. The odour of your ointments is above all aromatic spices. How much it means to me to see the Lord of majesty showing himself in physical movements and human feelings, not like the strong but like the weak. How much this strengthens me in my infirmity.

Spiritual flowers of divine peace

Happy is he who opens his heart to you, good Jesus, for you will enter to feed and rest there at noontime. Your coming, Lord, brings the midday of heavenly light to the chaste breast, calming every emotion of the heart with the infusion of divine peace. You strew the bed upon which you lie with spiritual flowers and adornments, so that the soul perceiving your presence and the sweetness of that sudden peace utters with wondrous love a cry of exultation and joy: You are beautiful, my beloved, and comely, our bed is covered with flowers.

The inconstancy of my mind

I pray that I may take up your cross and follow you. And if I wish to know how to follow you, your answer will be a question: 'How did you wander from me?' To this I answer that it was not by walking away on my feet, but by the inconstancy of my mind. Not wishing to give my soul wholly to you, I kept it to myself. Hoping to be my own master, I lost possession of myself. My life became a burden, and within me I found nothing but darkness and wretchedness, fear and need. Then I said to myself: I know what I must do. I will go to my my Father and tell him that I have sinned against heaven, and before him.

Healing perfumes

Your life on earth draws me as the perfume of the beloved attracts the lover. They are fragrant indeed, those ointments of yours, and they heal the sick, strengthen the weak, and gladden the sorrowing. The fragrance of your power draws me to follow you, and gives me new life by its salve. I shall follow you, O Lord, even though I cannot walk with you upon the flower-scented hills where your beloved spouse finds you, nor can I enter the garden where your body was buried. But let my flesh be buried with you, dearest Lord, in that garden, for I wish to live not for myself, but only for you who delivered yourself up for me.

Grace shatters darkness

How often, my Jesus, does day decline to evening, how often does intolerable grief follow some little consolation as a night mist obscures the daylight. Everything turns to ennui, everything I see is a burden. If anyone speaks, I scarcely listen. If anyone knocks, I scarcely hear. My heart is hard as flint, my tongue sticks, my eyes are drained dry. What then? I go out to the field to meditate, I open the sacred book, I am writing down my thoughts when suddenly, as Rebecca coming to meet me, your grace, good Jesus, shatters the darkness with daylight, dispels the ennui, and relieves the tension. Soon tears follow sighs, and heavenly joy accompanies the tears.

I commend my spirit

For the love of Christ, hasten. Release me, let me go free to him, whom I see before me, the King of Glory. What do you linger for? What do you? What are you waiting for? Hasten, for the love of Christ, hasten.

You are my God and my Lord, you are my refuge and my Saviour. You are my glory and my hope for evermore. Into your hands I commend my spirit.

Acknowledgements

We are grateful to the following publishers for permission to reprint copyright material.

CASSELL PLC
The Mirror of Charity. Translated and arranged by Geoffrey Webb and Adrian Walker. A.R. Mowbray & Co. Ltd., 1962.

CISTERCIAN PUBLICATIONS INC
WMU Station, Kalamazoo, Michigan 49008, U.S.A.
Treatises and The Pastoral Prayer, 1971, containing *Jesus at the Age of Twelve* translated by Theodore Berkeley OCSO; *A Rule of Life for a Recluse* translated by Mary Paul Macpherson OCSO; *The Pastoral Prayer* translated by R. Penelope Lawson CSMV.

ST PIETERSABDIJ
Prayers of St Aelred. Selected and introduced by A. Hoste, 1965.

The Cistercian Fathers Series, produced by Cistercian Publications, currently has three books of Aelred's works in print: *Treatises and the Pastoral Prayer, Spiritual Friendship* and *Dialogue on the Soul. The Mirror of Charity* should be available in the same series in 1990.

THE LAMP VISION OF . . . SERIES

LAMENT AND LOVE: THE VISION OF GEORGE HERBERT

Edited by Robert Van de Weyer

The first book in the Lamp Vision of . . . series is an anthology of extracts from the work of the great seventeenth century poet and parson. The extracts are especially chosen to define his unique Christian vision.

I STEP, I MOUNT: THE VISION OF JOHN HENRY NEWMAN

Edited by Robert Van de Weyer and Pat Saunders

In this selection of extracts, with an extended biographical introduction, we look at the life, ideas and poetry of Cardinal Newman. An Anglican for the first half of his life, Newman became the spiritual leader of the Oxford Movement, seeking sacramental renewal in the Anglican Church. In 1845, he became a Roman Catholic and set out to raise the importance of the laity in the eyes of that church.